WEIGHT LIFTING ESSENTIALS

Dedication

This is dedicated to Alice Steen and Cynthia Condon. The book you're holding would not exist without the unconditional love and support these two provided the authors throughout the years.

Thank you for everything, Mom.

Preface

This book has one main objective: To teach you the most effective, time-efficient way to lift weights—the best way to shed fat and build healthy muscle.

I've perfected this system over the past 17 years, working with every kind of client you can imagine. Middle-aged and older men and women looking to fit better in their clothes; obese individuals whose doctors told them they need to lose weight; competitive bodybuilders; high school and college athletes; and many more. This flexible system was born and raised by my 43,000 hours (and counting!) training clients.

Your program will be unique--just like you. But the fundamentals remain the same. The information contained in this course will be the foundation from which you can build your dream body upon.

Whether your goal is to compete at the highest levels, or just drop a few jean sizes, this system will save you countless hours.

Before now this information was only available to my physical clients at $125 per session or online for $1,000. I'm happy I've found a more affordable way to distribute this life-changing information to you. It's my sincere hope that this discount does not devalue the content in your mind.

Trust me: The hours of frustration and stagnation you're going to save yourself from are worth at least four figures.

Thank you for investing in your health. I'm honored and humbled to help you along your journey.

We're better together!

Sincerely,

Darin Steen

Father

Arnold's Next Great Trainer 2015

Head Coach and Owner of the Transformation Station

"NOTHING CAN STOP THE MAN WITH THE RIGHT MENTAL ATTITUDE FROM ACHIEVING HIS GOAL; NOTHING ON EARTH CAN HELP THE MAN WITH THE WRONG MENTAL ATTITUDE."
—THOMAS JEFFERSON

Josh N.

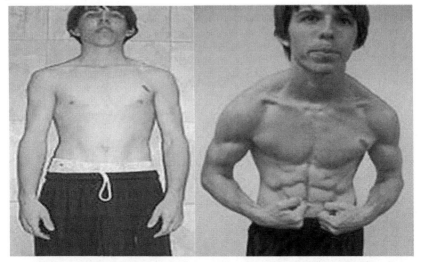

☑ *Gained 8 lbs of muscle and 1 and ½ inches on his arms*

☑ *Melted 10 lbs of fat off and 2 and ½ inches off his waist*

"I never thought I could be muscular with ripped abs. It was crazy how my body changed utilizing Darin's unique Slow Go methods."

Legal Stuff

The information contained in this book is for general guidance on matters of interest only. The application and impact of this information can vary widely based on the specific facts involved. Given the changing nature of laws, rules and regulations, and the inherent hazards of electronic communication, there may be delays, omissions or inaccuracies in information contained in this course. Accordingly, the information in this course is provided with the understanding that the authors and publishers are not herein engaged in rendering legal, medical, or other professional advice and services. As such, it should not be used as a substitute for consultation with professional legal, medical, or other competent advisers.

Consult your physician before starting any exercise program. Consult your physician prior to using any supplement if you are pregnant, nursing, taking medication, or have a medical condition. Discontinue use 2 weeks prior to surgery. Supplement claims have not been evaluated by the Food and Drug Administration. Supplements are not intended to diagnose, treat, cure, or prevent any disease.

While we have made every attempt to ensure that the information contained in this course has been obtained from reliable sources, Darin Steen is not responsible for any errors or omissions, or for the results obtained from the use of this information. All information in this site is provided "as is", with no guarantee of completeness, accuracy, timeliness or of the results obtained from the use of this information, and without warranty of any kind, express or implied, including, but not limited to warranties of performance, merchantability and fitness for a particular purpose. In no event will Darin Steen, his related partnerships or corporations, or the partners, agents or employees thereof be liable to you or anyone else for any decision made or action taken in reliance on the information in this course or for any consequential, special or similar damages, even if advised of the possibility of such damages.

Certain links in this course connect to other websites maintained by third parties over whom Darin Steen has no control. Darin Steen makes no representations as to the accuracy or any other aspect of information contained in other websites.

Contents

GETTING STARTED

Belief

"WHETHER YOU THINK YOU CAN, OR YOU THINK YOU CAN'T, YOU'RE RIGHT." —HENRY FORD

Belief is so important. You take a giant step towards your goals when you start to believe you can achieve them.

Now I can quote dozens of different studies and talk about the indisputable Placebo Effect. But I'd rather we save both of us time and you take my word for it.

Believe me. You have to believe in yourself.

You have what it takes to completely transform yourself.

Emotional Reason

"THE MYSTERY OF HUMAN EXISTENCE LIES NOT JUST IN STAYING ALIVE, BUT IN FINDING SOMETHING TO LIVE FOR."
—FYODOR DOSTOYEVSKY

Attach an emotional reason to belief and you're halfway to your goal.

Why do you want to transform your body? And what's the reason for that reason? Does that reason maybe even have a deeper reason?

The deeper you can go, the stronger you connect with a reason, the easier it will be for you. This system requires pushing your limits, and that's always easier when you are driven by a powerful Why.

Take some time, be thoughtful, and find your deepest one.

Pain Reframe

"HE WHO LEARNS MUST SUFFER."
—AESCHYLUS

According to many people who study the psychology of success—including Tony Robbins, a personal hero of mine—your brain only responses to two things: Pain and Pleasure.

Unfortunately it's an imperfect system. Messages get crossed or misinterpreted. And our brains aren't naturally good at playing the long-game. They seek instant gratification.

But the good news is: You can train your brain!

You can start associating lifting with the results, the compliments you get, the way you look and feel in your clothes, instead of the brief muscular pain you go through to get these pleasures.

Once you reframe how you view pain, you've completely changed the game...

After you've thoroughly visualized the long-term benefits—picturing in HD how much better the new you will look, feel, think, and act—it's time to take a cold hard look at the present and recent past.

What are you doing now that's preventing you from reaching your vision? What habits have you developed to get short-term pleasure while causing long-term pain?

The most common answers to these questions are: drinking, smoking, overeating, and undereating. We find something that gives us some type of reward—some pleasure. But we know, in the long-run, these habits are causing us pain and preventing us from being our best.

The key in all this? Habits.

***

Habits are a critical root of our behavior. Habits can save us time, energy, and precious mental bandwidth. Unfortunately not all habits fall into this category. Some are dangerous— even deadly.

According to the latest research, habits follow a three-step process:

- ☑ *Cue. A trigger that tells your brain to go into automatic mode and which habit to use.*
- ☑ *Routine. This can be physical or mental or emotional. Your brain believes this to be the best way to get to step 3.*
- ☑ *Reward. Rewards for a particular routine help your brain figure out whether or not this sequence is worth remembering.*

This *habit-loop* is the Rosetta's Stone of behavior change. Simply understanding how habits work—cue, routine, reward—makes them easier to control. But let's dig deeper.

Change, Not Deletion

Once a habit has formed, it can never be extinguished. That kind of sucks. But there is a silver lining: **You can change a habit.**

How does this work? In order to change an old habit, you must address the underlying craving.

Cravings are what make cues and rewards work. They power the habit loop. **To successful change a habit we must identify**

which craving is driving the behavior. To change an old habit, you have to address this craving. Keep the same cues and rewards as before, but feed the craving with a new routine.

STEP ONE

So what's our first step?

Awareness.

To change a habit we have to identify what triggers our habitual behavior. This isn't always easy, but it is a necessary step in changing our behavior. **Recognizing the cues and rewards driving our behavior is half the battle.**

After we have identified the cues, rewards, and the underlying craving fueling our unwanted routine, it's time to experiment with replacement routines. If you were thorough and honest enough with yourself in step one, this should be relatively straightforward. Insert the new routine into the old habit loop.

For some habits there is one more necessary ingredient: Belief. In many studies belief was the X factor that made a reworked habit loop into a permanent behavior.

Remember: Whether you think you can, or you think you can't, you're right.

The Buddy System

Communities are great at fostering belief. This is the primary reason for the success of AA and other support groups. A community of believers is stronger than a lone wolf. It can keep you on track when you feel like going off the rails. Whenever possible find a supportive tribe.

Habit Change Summary

First, identify the cue (trigger), reward, and underlying craving. Next, come up with an alternative routine that you believe will satisfy the underlying craving. Then implement the new routine. Simple. But simple and easy are not the same thing.

***

Visualize the beneficial effects of playing the long-game. Do it often—keep the desire for that positive pleasure burning strong. Replace toxic routines with winning ones.

New frame, new game!

Work

"Your dreams don't work unless you do."
— John C. Maxwell

Now, one more meta message before we dive into the nitty gritty.

Work. It's the key variable of success. I saved it for last because it's so important. Belief and emotional engagement get you halfway, work takes you the rest of the way to your goals.

It's not about perfection. Perfection paralyzes. It's about consistency. If you consistently put in the work you'll smash your plateaus and achieve amazing results.

You can't climb the ladder of success with your hands in your pockets. You can't get a hit if you don't swing the bat.

So climb. Swing. Relish the missteps and strikeouts; they're proof you're pushing your limits and growing. Enjoy the journey, for the journey is everything, my friend.

Don't just read this book.

Study it. Dissect it.

Practice the movements. Practice the movements. Practice the movements until they become engrained in your nervous system.

Put in the work.

Remember Arnold's most important secret to success: "None of my rules work, unless you do."

*"*ONLY I CAN CHANGE MY LIFE. NO ONE CAN DO IT FOR ME." —CAROL BURNETT*

Emily S.

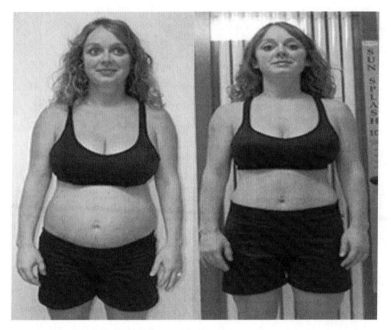

☑ *Melted 26 lbs. of fat and 7 ½ inches off her stomach*
☑ *Gained 4 lbs. of muscle*

I never tried to lose fat by lifting weights. The concept was very intriguing to me. I am so glad I gave it a try. I am hooked for life.

SLOW GO SYSTEM

Tempo

"How you do anything is how you do everything." —Tim Ferriss

Tempo—the speed in which you perform these exercises—is the most important pillar of my system. We have to slow down the repetition speed in order to speed up our progress.

It's counter-intuitive, I know. Clients struggle with this for a couple different reasons.

Guys—and in this case it's almost always guys—that have some experience lifting don't want to lift lighter weights. Maybe it's a pride thing. But all of them incorrectly assume that heavier is always better, that quantity outweighs rep quality.

Quality is so important, people. If you know how to properly generate force, you'll be safer and get stronger faster.

And the quantity we want to focus on is time under tension. Concentrating on how long your muscle is resisting a moderately heavy load, instead of how much weight you can whip around, will work better and save you hours in the gym.

The other most common client struggle is the polar opposite. These well-intended people are generally trying to "Just lose a little fat."

Many in this camp avoid weight training altogether. They think they'll get big and bulky if they lift weights.

This is just not true! I promise: Gaining bodybuilder muscles takes a lot of time and dedication to eating a ton of clean calories almost every day. Muscle only takes up about a quarter of the space fat does. So, if you want to, you're still able to slim down while gaining muscle.

Gaining muscle is the best way to lose fat because the more muscle you have, the more calories you burn at rest. So you turn your body into a fat burning machine.

That's why my system, built around the unique tempo you're about to learn, works for anyone. You can gain as much muscle as you want in the shortest amount of time. Either to slim down and firm up, or pack on a bunch of muscle (over time and with a high daily caloric intake!).

***

Like most things that work, this tempo is simple. It's a 1-3-1-3 rhythm. Start your set with a controlled exertion (positive); hold at the top for a one-second isometric squeeze; then take a full 3 seconds to return the weight(s) to its starting position (negative); repeat.

That's it. If you start to implement just this pillar in your workouts, I would give odds that you'll notice a significant improvement in your results.

I know in writing this may not be easily graspable—we're visual creatures. The HD photos in the exercise library of this book help illustrate further. The videos provide even richer visuals. Finally, I have a ton of free content on the web demonstrating proper tempo.

Tempo naturally helps strength the mind-muscle connection, another important pillar of the Slow Go System.

Mind-Muscle Connection

"Do not dwell in the past, do not dream of the future, concentrate the mind on the present moment." —Buddha

Connecting your mind to your muscles as closely as possible is another pillar of the Slow Go System designed to help you take it to the next level. Proprioception—awareness of one's body in space—is a key factor of how well we move our bodies.

If you're working with a coach or partner, that person can actually physically reinforce the mind-muscle connection.

It's as simple as having that person lightly tap the muscles you're currently working. If I tap the lateral heads of your triceps while you're doing cable pressdowns your mind will automatically home in on that muscle.

Alone it's got to be purely mental, but it can still have a powerful impact on making progress.

Laser-focus on the body part that's doing most of the work. Visualize contracting that muscle to where it's like squeezing water out of a sponge. Or create your own visualization to help you keep all of your concentration on your working muscles.

The more you can connect your mind with your muscle, the safer and stronger you become.

Breathing

*"*Whenever I feel blue, I start breathing again.*" —*L. Frank Baum

Breathing. How you breathe is so important. Yogis have held the breath to be sacred for thousands of years for good reason. Oxygen is power.

A lot of beginner and intermediate lifters struggle with practicing proper breathing. It's understandable. Your nervous system is trying to learn or ingrain a new movement. Adding synchronized breathing is one more thing to remember.

It's difficult at first—but worth it. Proper breathing will help you lift safer and have more power.

The worst thing you can do is hold your breath. Please make sure you're breathing while lifting. Holding your breath can lead to aneurysms and other nasty stuff. Breathe!

Optimal breathing occurs when you're exhaling during exertion and inhaling during the negative. If this sounds complicated, don't worry. You can find free videos explaining breathing (and tempo) on my YouTube channel.

Remember: Oxygen is power. Breathing properly is a key pillar to this system.

It's simple. It just takes awareness, practice, and patience.

Pulses (Micro-Reps)

"Put your heart, mind, and soul into even your smallest acts. This is the secret of success." —Swami Sivananda

Pulses—or micro-reps—are another important piece of the Slow Go system.

Ending your last repetition with two to four quarter-reps is a great way to squeeze out every last drop of value from the set.

Again, safety is the most important thing. A lot of exercises you will need a spotter to safely implement pulses.

To get the most out of your workout, make sure to utilize micro-reps whenever you can safely do so.

Failure

"THE MASTER HAS FAILED MORE TIMES THAN
THE BEGINNER HAS EVEN TRIED."
—STEPHEN MCCRANIE

Embracing failure is another key component of my Slow Go System.

We need to reframe how you see the number of reps you do. Yes, there is a range you want to aim for. But there isn't a magical number where if you hit it you'll see results.

The magic happens at the point of muscular failure. When your mind wants to quit but you force yourself to do a couple more reps.

These reps are what trigger real muscle growth. Not pushing till failure is a waste of a set and your time.

The need to push to this pain point is what makes belief and emotional reason so important. You'll need solid motivation to constantly push yourself to failure.

That's why training with a partner or coach is smart. A good partner or coach will help push you till true failure—and even past it with negatives.

Alone or with a partner, it's important to put safety first. Push yourself to muscular discomfort and failure, but no further. If you start to experience skeletal or joint pain, stop and consult your healthcare provider. Always use a spot on exercises where failure could be dangerous alone, such as bench press.

Fail fast, fail often, fail forward.

"OUR GREATEST WEAKNESS LIES IN GIVING UP. THE MOST CERTAIN WAY TO SUCCEED IS ALWAYS TO TRY JUST ONE MORE TIME."
—THOMAS EDISON

Jason B.

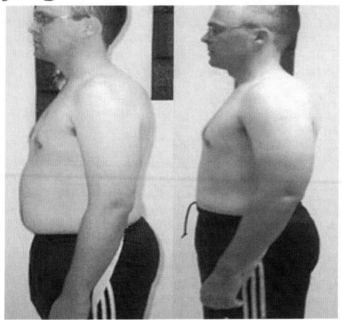

☑ *Melted 26 lbs. of fat and 5 inches off his stomach*

☑ *Gained 9 lbs. of muscle and ½ inch on each arm*

Darin's unique methods fit into my crazy-busy schedule. I have so much more energy and self-confidence now. I never lifted weights before. If I can change my body, anyone can. Go for it!

LEG EXERCISES

Walking Lunges

This is one of the best leg exercises there is—when done correctly. From the starting position, with feet side by side, stride forward with your right foot. Make stride long and put weight on the heel of the front foot.

While exaggerating your strong, tall posture and leaning back, bend left knee and descend toward floor. Very lightly tap knee on floor and explode up. Drive your left foot passed your right foot and stride all the way through to the next step.

Once foot hits floor, keep weight on the heel of your front foot and descend slowly toward floor with right knee. Very lightly tap knee on floor and explode up. Drive right foot passed your left foot and stride all the way through your next step.

Walk like this for about 30-45 feet. On your last stride tap back knee on floor with three light taps—or pulses—before driving up. This technique is very intense.

Dumbbell Squats

Starting Position:

Take one dumbbell in each hand; stand tall with strong posture and feet shoulder-width apart.

Inhale. Drive your glutes and hamstrings back behind you like you are sitting down in a chair. Keep your body weight on your heels.

Keeping good posture, descend until the top of your thighs are slightly below parallel to the floor. Then exhale as you stand up, driving your bodyweight through your heels.

Bad Form:

Do not round your back or lean forward.

Hamstring Curls

Starting Position:

This is my favorite hamstring exercise. Position yourself on the bench face-down, with your knees hanging a couple inches off the edge of the bench. Set dumbbell on floor, leaning against a short platform.

From starting position, drive toes upward and lift dumbbell to top position.

The key to this exercise is to constantly squeeze the knees together. Act like there is a hundred-dollar bill between your knees, and if you keep it there, you get to keep the cash after the set. Keep the toes pointed slightly up. Breathing in and squeezing the knees together, lower the feet and the dumbbell. Bring feet and dumbbell down so legs are slightly above parallel to floor.

While slowly exhaling, squeeze knees together and drive dumbbell to top position. With a little bit of practice you will be able to hold the dumbbell in between the feet with no problem.

This exercise will isolate the hamstrings unlike any machine.

Bad Form:

It is very important to force hips and pelvis to stay down on the pad.

Smith Box Squats

Starting Position:

Stand tall with strong posture and place bar on your traps. A Smith Machine is a safer alternative to free weights.

Initiate descent by driving glutes and hamstrings back, as if you are sitting back in a chair, as you inhale. Keep weight on your heels.

Lightly tap buns on box and drive up to starting position as you exhale.

Pulse Technique: tap buns lightly on box three times before exploding up on last two repetitions of each set.

Bad Form:

Do not put weight on the balls of your toes. Do not round out your back or look down.

Romanian (Stiff-Legged) Deadlifts

Starting Position:

Stand tall, open shoulder blades, and engage lower back. Focus on maintaining a strong, tall posture during the entire set.

While keeping legs stiff, bend at hips and drive your glutes back as the bar descends toward the floor. Make sure to keep the bar very close to your body. Breathe in as the bar moves toward floor.

Descend until bar is a few inches under your knees. Pause for one second. Exhale as you slowly return to starting position. Focus on keeping lower back tight and pushing through your heels. For an advanced technique, put your toes up on a platform about ½ to 1 inch high. This will force you to stand through your heels.

Bad Form:

Do not go too low and round out your lower back.

One-Legged Dumbbell Squats

Starting Position:

Stand on box with strong, neutral posture. Hold dumbbell on side of working leg, lift non-squatting knee in air. The leg on the box is the working leg. To help with balance put free hand on the side of your head. Try not to push off with the back leg. Focus on just using the working leg to lift your body's weight.

Drive non-working leg back and plant on floor as you inhale.
Bend knee and descend slowly.

Tap knee lightly on floor and explode back up to starting position as you exhale. Keep good posture and drive up though your working heel.

This is an excellent exercise.

Bad Form:

Do not lean forward. Keep front knee behind toe and weight on your front heel.

Reverse Barbell Lunges

Starting Position:

This is maybe my favorite hamstrings and glutes exercise. Place barbell on upper back. Stand tall, chest open, blades back, and tighten lower back.

Stride forward with right foot. Keep body weight on heel of front foot. Bend back leg knee and slowly descend to floor.

Make sure to keep your weight on your heel and the knee well behind your toe. Very lightly tap back knee on floor and aggressively (controlled aggression) push off right foot. The goal is to get back to original starting position. At first you may not be able to push off hard enough to make it all the way back to the starting position. But start with a light weight (maybe just the bar) and you will improve in no time.

Finish Position:

This is a very challenging exercise. Stick with it and before you know it, you will have the ability to perform it flawlessly. It is one of the best at shaping and firming the buns. The foot that you are stepping forward with and pushing off of is the hamstring and bun that you are working. Finish all reps with one leg, then switch and work the other leg.

Stationary Box Lunge

Starting Position:

Start with back leg up on box. Working leg is front leg. Stand tall with good strong posture. Make sure to keep weight on front foot heel.

Initiate movement by driving buns and hips back as if you are
sitting in chair. Descend as you inhale.

Keeping good posture, tap knee lightly and exhale as you drive through front foot heel to the starting position.

Complete one set to failure for each leg.

Bad Form:

Do not lean forward. Keep front knee behind toe and keep body weight on heel.

"IT ALWAYS SEEMS IMPOSSIBLE UNTIL IT'S DONE." —NELSON MANDELA

Dalia L.

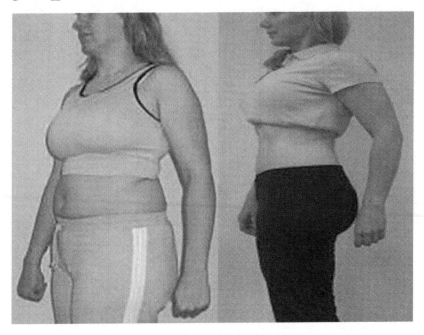

☑ *Melted 36 lbs and over 7 inches off her waist and 6 inches off her hips*

☑ *Gained 4 lbs of muscle*

Darin's program was so doable. It amazed me how time efficient it was. I am so happy I got my body and life back after kids.

BACK EXERCISES

Pull-ups and Chin-ups

Starting Position:

Grip is shoulder-width apart. Walk up to bar with a 90° angle in your elbow joint and grab bar. Do not fall into the trap of thinking that a wider hand placement on the bar will make your back wider. Doing so will make the exercise less effective. Cue clients—or yourself—to create torque by telling them to "bend the bar" or handle outward.

Slowly take feet off floor by bending legs (keep bent during exercise). Focus on stretching the scapula.

Take a deep breath in then, looking slightly upward, exhale as you open up the chest by pulling your body up.

Pause for one second at the top. Visualize that you are driving your elbows through the floor.

This is one of the most effective back exercises there is.

Even if you can only do 3 or 4 high-quality reps, stick with it. If you're not there yet, start on an assisted pull-up machine. If you have a partner have them push up on legs to aid for a couple extra reps.

Deadlift

Starting position:

The deadlift is one of the most functional exercises. It works the entire posterior chain, from your neck to your calves. The grip should be staggered with one palm up and one down. Grip is just wide enough to fit the knees in between elbows. Take a breath in and lean back on your heels and stand as you exhale.

Keep the lower back tight by keeping chest open and shoulder blades back. By understanding torque, this is relatively easy. Throughout the exercise you want to mentally remind yourself to maintain external rotation at the shoulders and hips.

At the top make sure to keep the hips underneath the shoulders. This is where you can really squeeze the upper back and traps for three seconds in between reps. To start the next rep drive the glutes back like you are sitting down in a chair. Feel your weight through your heels as you descend and breathe in. Tap the floor with the weight lightly and execute the next rep.

Bad Form:

Do not lean forward or look down. Keep the weight back on your heels.

This can be a great exercise to strengthen the entire back side of your body, primarily your lower back. But only when it's performed correctly.

One-Arm Dumbbell Row

Start Position:

Use an incline bench for best body position. Tighten lower back by rotating hips and sticking buns high into the air. Dumbbell heads are at 9 and 3 o'clock. Left knee and elbow are on the right edge of bench (when doing right-handed rows).

As you exhale drive the dumbbell up close to your ribcage. Dumbbell heads turn to 12 and 6 o'clock. Keep elbow tight to body as you drive. Return dumbbell to start position as you inhale.

Bad Form:

Make sure not to flatten buns out and do not round lower back.

Close-Grip Pulldowns

Starting Position:

Lean forward a bit and stretch your scapula. This stretch phase of back exercises is a very important part of each repetition. Make sure you do not skip it.

Sit up tall, drive chest and abdominals forward and exhale. I tell my clients not to think about pulling the handle down to your chest; rather, think about sitting up tall, opening your chest, and driving your sternum bone up to the ceiling. Think of it as a strong posture move.

Pause for one second at the bottom, isometrically squeezing your upper back muscles.

Bad Form:

Do not lean back. Lighten up weight so that you can lean forward and into the pull down machine.

CHEST EXERCISES

Dumbbell Chest Press

Starting Position: Sit on the edge of a bench. Pin your elbows tight to the side of your body. As you rock back, bring your thighs and the dumbbells with you as you lay down on the bench. Then bring your legs and feet down to the floor and get ready for the first repetition.

Keep your chest open and shoulder blades close together. Always keep three points of contact, your feet on the floor, your buns, and your shoulder blades. Someone should be able to slide their hand between the bench and the small of your back. As you exhale, slowly drive the dumbbells to the top and pause for one second.

Slowly separate and lower the bells as you inhale.

The bells should face each other slightly at the top and at the bottom.

Do not kick your elbows back behind your head on the descent. At the bottom pause for one second, feeling the chest muscles stretch, then exhale and drive bells to top position.

Bad Form:

When you get fatigued your chest will want to cave in; your hips and head will want to rise off bench. As soon as any of these occur end the set slowly and safely.

Barbell Chest Press

Start/Finish:

Make sure to keep your feet, buns, and shoulder blades in contact with the floor and bench. Do not grip the bar too wide, as this will put excess stress on your shoulder joints. But do not grip bar too narrow, as this will put excess stress on your wrists.

Bring the bar down slowly as you inhale. Maintain that mindset—slow and steady wins the race—as you both lower and raise the bar. You'll have to keep the weight lighter, but you will get a better workout with this type of mindset.

Stop the bar for one second as it lightly touches your chest. Then exhale as you drive the bar to the top position. During the entire duration of the set focus on keeping your chest open, shoulder blades back, and your lower back arched while maintaining the 3 points of contact with the floor and bench.

Dumbbell Fly

Starting Position:

This chest exercise is similar but slightly different than the press. It's more of a stretching movement. Use a weight that is considerably less than your press weight. Again, chest open, blades back, and lower back arched away from bench. Bells are just slightly facing each other.

As you start to lower the dumbbells turn the palms toward each other. With a slight bend in the elbow, bring the dumbbells away from your body to the bottom position.

At the bottom position pause for one second. Then start to drive the dumbbells to the top with the mindset of wrapping your arms around an oak tree.

Bad Form:

Do not lower the bells and the arms too low. Doing so will put a strain on the ball-and- socket (shoulder) joints. Do not lower elbows below bench.

Medicine Ball Pushups

Starting position:

This is an excellent chest exercise that works your balance and stability muscles. Make sure you keep medicine balls in the butt of your palm. Keep your body nice and rigid.

Slowly breathing in, lower to the bottom position and pause for one second. On the decent focus on your elbows slightly coming in toward the body. Focus on the stretch at the bottom. Then exhale and slowly drive back up to the starting position.

For you more advanced clients, simply put the feet up on a bench to intensify this exercise. As you get stronger you can put your feet up higher. The higher your feet, the more challenging the set.

Bad Form:

As soon as you do not have the ability to keep your body stiff and tight, end the set by softly setting your hips and thighs on the floor

"THE PAST CANNOT BE CHANGED. THE FUTURE IS YET IN YOUR POWER." —UNKNOWN

Hank B.

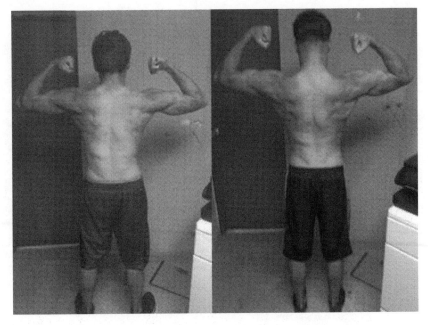

☑ *In only 6 weeks: Gained 5.12 lbs. of muscle and lost 2.93 lbs. of fat*

☑ *Gained 1 inch on each arm and gained over 2 inches on his chest*

Before Darin's program I tried everything to gain weight size. His unique Slow Go technique not only works well to get stronger and gain muscle mass, it also is safer on my joints.

AB EXERCISES

Planks

Starting Position:

Face down on mat. Keep elbows directly under shoulders. Make sure to look up slightly and keep neck straight. This is an isometric hold. Keep body as stiff and straight as possible. Pull your belly button back toward spine and away from waistband on shorts. Draw your lower pelvic muscles up high. Do a keegle squeeze—it is like trying to stop urine in the middle of flow.

This is a great exercise for all the deep core muscles of the midsection. With this exercise you literally can decrease the size of your waist by strengthening your deepest midsection muscle your Transverse Abdominas (TVA). When your TVA is stronger it will support your back better and hold your guts in tighter. When your TVA is stronger your waistline will decrease. It's like having a pair of those shaping underwear they sell on late-night television. Work up to holding each set for 90 seconds.

Turn on side and put elbow directly under shoulder. Put top leg foot in front of bottom leg foot, heel to toe. Put top arm hand on side oblique muscles to feel and focus on target area. Open chest up and focus on keeping posture tall and straight. This is a great exercise for tightening up your love handles.

This can be an isometric exercise or you can pulse your top hip up slightly toward ceiling to intensify focus in obliques. Range of motion is only an inch or two. Focus on only the side obliques that are closest to the floor. In the picture, I am working my left side. For each set shoot for 20 slow, methodical pulses. Once you are done with one side, flip over and work opposite side.

Bad Form:

Do not let your buns come up and lower back round out. 15 seconds of good form is more effective than 90 seconds of bad form.

Med Ball V Situps

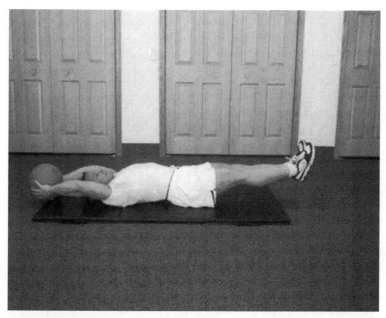

Starting Position:

Hold medicine ball above head with arms stiff. Straighten legs and keep feet about one foot off floor. Tilt hips and flatten lower back into floor.

Keeping legs, arms, and torso stiff, quickly drive chin to chest and raise upper body and legs off floor and balance on buns for one second.

Pull med ball into naval and knees up to ball and isometrically squeeze core tight for three seconds. Slowly return to starting position and repeat.

Alternate technique:

From starting position come up to second position. Instead of pulling ball and knees in toward naval, slowly twist shoulders to each side as you lower ball to floor. Make sure to keep arms stiff and twist slowly, and hold as ball taps floor for 3 seconds. Try to keep heels off floor during.

Reverse Sit-Ups

Starting Position:

Lay back on bench. Grab back of bench behind head with both hands and put a 90° angle in both knees. Tilt hips and force lower back flat to bench.

Keep a 90° angle in both knees during entire exercise. From starting position lower legs. Do not drop feet below bench height.

As you exhale slowly drive knees up to ceiling. Put your mind in your lower abs as you drive your buns and lower back off bench up to ceiling. Pause in this position for two seconds. Keep abs tight and inhale as you slowly lower to starting position. Before each rep, lower legs from starting position first, then slowly drive knees to ceiling.

Bad Form:

Do not come up to high. This will take tension off of lower abdominals and put into lower back.

Multi-Dimensional Crunches

Starting Position:

Lay flat on back, bend knees, and place feet about one foot away from buns. Arms are stiff. Place one hand over the top of the other. Tilt your hips (flat buns) and feel lower back get flat to pad.

Drive chin toward chest and bring shoulder blades off pad as you exhale.

Come to top position and pause for two seconds. Focus on blowing air out and squeezing abdominal muscles as you continue to push your lower back through the floor. Go slow with this one. 15 slow reps done properly are way more effective than 50 done fast. Go for quality versus quantity.

"WELL DONE IS BETTER THAN WELL SAID."
—BENJAMIN FRANKLIN

Wendy B.

☑ *Melted 30 lbs of fat—5 inches off her stomach and 4 inches off her hips*

☑ *Gained 5 lbs of muscle*

I feel like a totally new person with a new lease on life. I am proud of myself now and I feel like I am a much better mother and spouse. I am excited about my future.

Shoulder Exercises

Upright Rows

Starting Position:

Grab curl bar palms down (pronated grip) approximately 8-10 inches apart, thumbs on top by fingers. Stand with a neutral spine. Keep feet shoulder-width apart.

As you exhale pull bar to top position. The bar naturally arcs away from body at midpoint.

The bar touches body at top and bottom of movement. Make sure to keep elbows higher than hands. Pause for one second at the top, inhale, and slowly return to starting position.

Bad Form:

Do not lean forward and round your back.

Seated Arnold Presses

Starting Position:

Sit up tall with good posture. Keep dumbbells shoulder-height. Create torque (external rotation) in the shoulders. Do not bring bells lower than chin height.

Exhale and drive dumbbells to ceiling with palms facing forward. Drive thumbs slightly higher than pinkies. Pause for one second at top, touching dumbbells and squeezing shoulder muscles. Make sure not to lock elbows straight. Stop slightly short of full lockout.

Separate dumbbells and inhale on the way down back to starting position. Try not to look up as I did in this demo. Look straight ahead with a neutral neck.

Bad Form:

Do not let the weights come too low.

Standing Dumbbell Lateral Raises

Starting Position:

Stand in neutral spine, palms toward your body. Squeeze upper-body muscles tight. Keep slight bend in elbows.

As you exhale bring dumbbells up to top position. Arms are in between straight and a 90° angle in elbow. Do not let wrists droop. Lead with knuckles toward ceiling. Pause for one second in top position.

Dumbbells are slightly higher than shoulders. Remember to flex wrists so knuckles are up toward ceiling. Slowly return to the starting position.

Bad Form:

Do not lean back. This usually happens if you go too fast or if the weight is too heavy. You will lose focus off of the shoulders and risk injury to the lower back.

Military Press

Starting Position:

Grab curl-bar at widest grip. Sit up tall with good posture. If you have a seat with a foot rest, straighten legs to help lower back get snug to back rest. Create and maintain torque in the shoulders. Look up and keep bar right under chin.

As you exhale, drive bar through ceiling.

To isolate shoulder muscles better, as bar passes chin, start to look straight ahead. Stop short of full lockout and pause for one second. Then inhale as you bring bar down slowly to starting position.

Standing Barbell Press

Starting Position:

Stand tall with strong posture, feet shoulder-width apart. Look up and keep bar under chin close to neck. Do not let bar come lower than shoulders. Bend knees slightly and exhale as you drive bar up toward the ceiling.

As the bar passes chin look straight ahead.

Pause at top for one second with slight bend in elbows. Inhale as bar descends to starting position. Look up slightly so bar will not hit head.

Bad Form:

Do not lean back. Doing so will injure lower back.

"WHEN I LET GO OF WHAT I AM, I BECOME WHAT I MIGHT BE." —LAO TZU

Joe M.

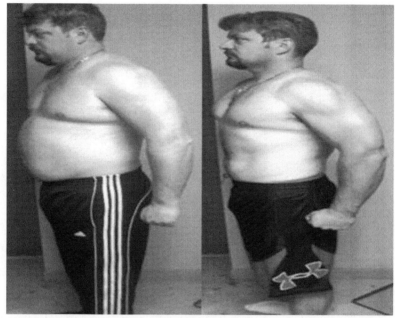

☑ *Lost 36 lbs. of fat, gained 6 lbs of muscle, and slashed his overall BF% from 32.88 to 20.5*

☑ *Melted 10 inches of fat off his stomach and gained ½ an inch of muscle on each arm*

I am super busy with family and business. I never thought I had time to exercise. Darin's slow go system changed all that for me. It worked so well for me, after I graduated from his program I trained myself and easily maintained my body. Darin's program is a life changer.

Biceps Exercises

Standing EZ Bar Curls

Starting Position:

Grab curl bar. Get into neutral spine. A curl bar is safer on the wrists than a straight bar. Squeeze your grip very tight and lock your wrists stiff.

As you exhale push bar away from body and drive up toward ceiling. Keep upper arms pinned tight to your sides.

Isometrically squeeze biceps for two seconds. Stand tall and keep weight on your heels.

Bad Form:

Do not lean forward. This will injure your lower back. If you have to lean forward, the weight is too heavy. Lighten weight, go slow, and stand tall.

Standing Preacher Curls

Starting Position:

Bend knees and get armpits high on top of pad. Grab curl bar with narrow grip. Squeeze grip tight and keep wrists stiff. If you do not have a standing preacher bench, you can use a hyper extension bench turned backwards like I do. It works great.

As you inhale slowly lower the weight for a 3-second count.

Pause for 2 seconds at the bottom. If you do not have any pain in your elbows, allow arms to totally lengthen out. If you do have discomfort in the elbows, stop short of full lockout.

Exhale and slowly bring bar up to starting position. Do not bring bar to nose in top position as this will take tension off of biceps.

Seated Dumbbell Curls

Starting Position:

Keep strong posture with chest open and shoulder blades back. Keep dumbbells 6-12 inches away from body. Keep palms up toward the ceiling.

As you exhale drive dumbbells up to top position. Pause for two seconds and flex biceps. Do not come too high as this will take tension off of biceps. As you come up with dumbbells bring pinkie dumbbell head slightly higher than thumb. Push elbow back slightly and bring dumbbells down slowly to starting position, again keeping pinkie dumbbell higher than thumb.

Note: Offset grip toward pinkie DB head. This will aid in bringing pinkie DB head higher.

Alternate Grip:

Grab dumbbells with a hammer grip. They call it a hammer grip because it's like you are swinging a hammer. Palms do not face up, they face each other. Use same technique as described above for traditional palms up grip. The hammer grip works the lower biceps more.

Concentration Curls

Starting Position:

Sit on edge of bench with feet wide. Rest elbow of working arm on inside of thigh.

Note: Offset grip toward the pinkie dumbbell head. This will aid in bringing pinkie head higher.

As you exhale bring pinkie head of dumbbell slightly higher than thumb head.

Bring pinkie head to nose and isometrically squeeze biceps for two seconds before returning to the starting position.

Triceps Exercises

Seated Overhead Dumbbell Extensions

Starting Position:

Grab dumbbell with palms open to ceiling and thumbs wrapped around handle. Push dumbbell straight overhead. If your seat has a foot rest, straighten legs to help lower back feel support on back pad.

Bend wrists and keep palms parallel to ceiling. Dumbbell handle should stay perpendicular to floor. Lock elbows and isometrically squeeze triceps.

As you inhale bring dumbbell down to bottom position, keeping palms parallel to ceiling. Pause for one second then exhale slowly as you as you drive dumbbell up to starting position. You will feel the focus on the triceps better if you squeeze your elbows tight to your head throughout the entire set.

Bad Form:

Do not keep wrists straight and do not let elbows come away from head. Note dumbbell handle is not perpendicular to floor.

Cable Pressdowns

Starting Position:

Stand tall with good posture. Grab rope and push the base of your palms together. This will naturally help remind you to pin your elbows tight to the side of your body. Forearms should be slightly above parallel to floor. If you do not have a rope, a hand towel will work just as well. Simply pull towel though hook and grip at ends.

As you exhale, drive grip down to bottom position, keep fists pushed together. Do not let elbows flare out to sides.

In the bottom position separate fists. Isometrically squeeze triceps for two seconds as you attempt to tear rope apart. Visualize that you are trying to drive the knobs on the ends of the rope out to the walls on each side of you. Then as you inhale, drive fists together and slowly return to the starting position.

Standing EZ Bar Overhead Extensions

Starting Position:

Grab curl-bar with a narrow grip and hold bar directly over your head. Tighten up your core by pulling your belly button back away from the waist band on your shorts. Feet are shoulder-width apart. Keep slight bend in arms and isometrically squeeze your triceps.

As you inhale bring bar down slowly. The bar should come down right through the midline of your body. Look down slightly and bring head forward so you don't hit your head. This is one of the few triceps exercises that you should allow your elbows to naturally flare out. You do not have to pin the elbows tight toward your head.

In bottom position do not rest bar on neck. Exhale and slowly drive bar to top position. Keep grip very tight, focus on keeping wrists stiff and drive knuckles toward ceiling as bar rises. As bar passes head bring head up and look straight ahead at top position.

Skull Crushers

Starting Form:

Lay on bench with feet on floor and hold curl bar with narrow grip. Keep bar over eyes, lock arms stiff and isometrically squeeze your triceps. Squeeze grip tight and keep wrists stiff. As an alternate grip try putting your thumb on the same side of bar as fingers. This grip seems to take some focus off of the forearms.

As you inhale lower bar. Make sure to push bar behind you on the way down. Note bar is behind my hair line and not over eyes. The goal is to keep your upper arm (from shoulder to elbow) stationary during each set. To intensify focus in your triceps, squeeze elbows toward each other during entire set.

Unique Technique:

Lift your head off of bench and bring bar behind head. Pause for one second then exhale and return bar to top position. This is somewhat of an advanced technique that will allow you to get a deeper stretch in the triceps.

Bad Form:

Do not bring bar too far forward over chest during set. This will take tension out of triceps and put in chest and shoulders.

"ALWAYS DO YOUR BEST. WHAT YOU PLANT
NOW, YOU WILL HARVEST LATER."
—OG MANDINO

Bri N.

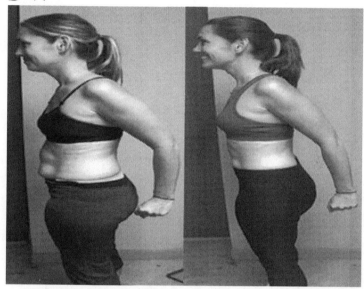

*In only 4 weeks: Melted 12 lbs. of fat—3 inches off her
stomach, 1 inch off each leg, and 3 inches off her hips*

Gained 3 lbs. of muscle

I never lifted weights before hiring Darin.
I was amazed at how my body seemed
to change every week. I have 2 small
children and no time. If I can do this
anyone can. I am amazed at how my
mental and emotional health improved,
too. That was a nice unexpected side
benefit.

Sample Workout Splits

Sample Workout Splits

Beginner / 3-day Split

Day One: Chest and Biceps

Day Two: Active Recovery/ Cardio

Day Three: Back and Triceps

Day Four: Active Recovery / Cardio

Day Five: Legs and Shoulders

Day Six: Active Recovery / Cardio

Day Seven: Rest

Intermediate / 4-day Split

Day One: Chest and Biceps

Day Two: Active Recovery/ Cardio

Day Three: Back and Triceps

Day Four: Active Recovery / Cardio

Day Five: Legs

Day Six: Shoulders

Day Seven: Rest

Day One: Chest and Biceps

10-20 minutes of warming up and mobilization.

Chest exercise [e.g. Chest Press] #1, set #1—use a relatively light weight to warmup, stretch, and really focus on form.

60-90 seconds of rest.

Biceps exercise [e.g. Preacher Curls] #1, set #1—use a relatively light weight to warmup, stretch, and really focus on form.

Chest exercise #1, set #2—use your working weight, a weight that is relatively heavy but still allows you to maintain control and good form throughout the exercise. Go till failure.

60-90 seconds of rest.

Biceps exercise #1, set #2—use your working weight. Go till failure.

Chest exercise #1, set #3—use your working weight. Go till failure, finishing the set with 2 pulses (micro-reps).

60-90 seconds of rest.

Biceps exercise #1, set #3—use your working weight. Go till failure, finishing the set with 2 pulses.

Ab exercise [e.g. Planks] or mobility exercise for 3-5 minutes.

Chest exercise [e.g. Flys] #2, set #1—use your working weight. Go till failure.

60-90 seconds rest.

Biceps exercise [e.g. Standing Curls] #2, set #1—use your working weight. Go till failure.

Ab exercise or mobility exercise for 3-5 minutes.

Chest exercise #2, set #2—use your working weight. Go till failure, finishing the set with 2 pulses.

Biceps exercise #2, set #2—use your working weight. Go till failure, finishing the set with 2 pulses.

10-20 minutes of walking or biking and stretching to (literally) cool down.

Day Three: Back and Triceps

10-20 minutes of warming up and mobilization.

Back exercise [e.g. Deadlift] #1, set #1—use a relatively light weight to warmup, stretch, and really focus on form.

60-90 seconds of rest.

Triceps exercise [e.g. Pressdowns] #1, set #1—use a relatively light weight to warmup, stretch, and really focus on form.

Back exercise #1, set #2—use your working weight, a weight that is relatively heavy but still allows you to maintain control and good form throughout the exercise. Go till failure.

60-90 seconds of rest.

Triceps exercise #1, set #2—use your working weight. Go till failure.

Back exercise #1, set #3—use your working weight. Go till failure, finishing the set with 2 pulses (micro-reps).

60-90 seconds of rest.

Triceps exercise #1, set #3—use your working weight. Go till failure, finishing the set with 2 pulses.

Ab exercise [e.g. Multi-Dimensional Crunches] or mobility exercise for 3-5 minutes.

Back exercise [e.g. Lat Pulldowns] #2, set #1—use your working weight. Go till failure.

60-90 seconds rest.

Triceps exercise [e.g. Extensions] #2, set #1—use your working weight. Go till failure.

Ab exercise or mobility exercise for 3-5 minutes.

Back exercise #2, set #2—use your working weight. Go till failure, finishing the set with 2 pulses.

60-90 seconds of rest.

Triceps exercise #2, set #2—use your working weight. Go till failure, finishing the set with 2 pulses.

10-20 minutes of walking or biking and stretching cooldown.

Day Five: Legs and Shoulders

10-20 minutes of warming up and mobilization.

Shoulder exercise [e.g. Standing Barbell Press] #1, set #1—use a relatively light weight to warmup, stretch, and really focus on form.

60-90 seconds of rest.

Leg exercise [e.g. Squats] #1, set #1—use a relatively light weight to warmup, stretch, and really focus on form.*

Shoulder exercise #1, set #2—use your working weight, a weight that is relatively heavy but still allows you to maintain control and good form throughout the exercise. Go till failure.

60-90 seconds of rest.

Leg exercise #1, set #2—use your working weight. Go till failure.

Shoulder exercise #1, set #3—use your working weight. Go till failure, finishing the set with 2 pulses (micro-reps).

60-90 seconds of rest.

Leg exercise #1, set #3—use your working weight. Go till failure, finishing the set with 2 pulses.

Ab exercise [e.g. Reverse Situps] or mobility exercise for 3-5 minutes.

Shoulder exercise [e.g. Arnold Presses] #2, set #1—use your working weight. Go till failure.

60-90 seconds of rest.

Leg exercise [e.g. Hamstring Curls] #2, set #1—use your working weight. Go till failure.

Ab exercise or mobility exercise for 3-5 minutes.

Shoulder exercise #2, set #2—use your working weight. Go till failure, finishing the set with 2 pulses.

60-90 seconds of rest.

Leg exercise #2, set #2—use your working weight. Go till failure, finishing the set with 2 pulses.

10-20 minutes of walking or biking and stretching cooldown.

* Doing standing barbell presses paired with squats is a fantastic combo. The presses activate your core and shoulders, leading to better form for squats.

4-Day Split Routine

"SIMPLICITY IS THE ULTIMATE SOPHISTICATION."
—LEONARDO DA VINCI

The 4-day routine is a natural progression from the 3-day split.

Days 1 and 3 remain the same. If you want to take it up a notch, you can add a working set to each exercise you perform.

Day 5 splits into 2 separate days, legs and shoulders. The flow and structure of the workout remains the same: 4 exercises working safely to failure on at least 2 sets with a warmup, cooldown, and core and mobility work.

If you still want to group exercises in 2 for efficiency you can. For shoulders, pair press exercises with shrugs or farmer's carriers—exercises that focus on the trap muscles. For legs, pair an exercise that focuses on the quads—like leg extensions— with an exercise that's primarily for hamstrings.

If you have any questions about this or anything else in the course, you can e-mail me at darin[at]fatlosslifestyle[dot]com with the subject line "WLE Question." I'll respond as soon as possible.

Closing Thoughts

Thank You

"As we express our gratitude, we must never forget that the highest appreciation is not to utter words, but to live by them." —John F. Kennedy

Thank you for taking this course. I sincerely hope you got a lot out of it.

If you did, a 5-star review would really help us get the Slow Go System to as many people as possible.

If you feel this course was anything less than 5-stars, please e-mail Darin[at]fatlosslifestyle[dot]com and let me know what would have made or could make it a 5 for you.

I hope you continue to use the Slow Go System, and make the rest of your life the best of your life!

P.S. If you are interested in taking the video course version of Weight Lifting Essentials, here is a link with an exclusive promo code for Amazon readers. [Softcover readers: the course's URL is http://udemy.com/weight-lifting-essentials and the promo code is "READERLEADER".]

Made in the USA
Lexington, KY
27 January 2018